Home & Away

Home & Away

The Old Town Poems

Kevin Miller

Pleasure Boat Studio: A Literary Press
New York

Home & Away: The Old Town Poems
© 2009 by Kevin Miller
ISBN 978-1-929355-48-8
Library of Congress Control Number: 2008930742

Design by Susan Ramundo
Cover by Jonas Lerman

Pleasure Boat Studio is a proud subscriber to the Green Press Initiative. This program encourages the use of 100% post-consumer recycled paper with environmentally friendly inks for all printing projects in an effort to reduce the book industry's economic and social impact. With the cooperation of our printing company, we are pleased to offer this book as a Green Press book.

Pleasure Boat Studio books are available through the following:
SPD (Small Press Distribution) Tel. 800-869-7553, Fax 510-524-0852
Partners/West Tel. 425-227-8486, Fax 425-204-2448
Baker & Taylor Tel. 800-775-1100, Fax 800-775-7480
Ingram Tel. 615-793-5000, Fax 615-287-5429
Amazon.com and **bn.com**

and through
PLEASURE BOAT STUDIO: A LITERARY PRESS
www.pleasureboatstudio.com
201 West 89 Street
New York, NY 10024

Contact **Jack Estes**
Fax: 888-810-5308
Email: *pleasboat@gmail.com*

Acknowledgments

Grateful acknowledgment is made to the following magazines and presses where versions of these poems first appeared.

Beloit Poetry Journal, Cascade, Crab Creek Review, Cranky, DMQ Review, Gingko Tree Review, Literary Salt, Peasandcues Press Broadside Series, Plymouth Writer Anthology, Poetry Jumps Off the Shelf, Poetry Northwest, Pontoon, Seattle Review, String Town, Tacoma Arts Commission Broadside Series, The Burnside Review, Triton, Twaddle, Windfall, Voices on the Wind, zyzzyva

I am grateful for the Tacoma Artists Initiative Grant from The Tacoma Arts Commission, which assisted with the completion of this project.

My thanks to Barry Grimes, Derek Sheffield, Joseph and Marquita Green, Peasandcues Press, Allen Braden, Casey Fuller, Loren Sundlee, Jim and Karen Bodeen, Blue Begonia Press, Jonas Lerman, Vance Thompson, Kathi Morrison-Taylor, Dan Peters, Mike Robinson, King's Books, and Jack Estes.

For Cam

Small things make the past.
Make the present seem out of place.

—Eavan Boland

Table of Contents

I. HOME

Poem for Jonas Before Independence Day / 3
Near Spring, Old Town / 4
What the Day Provides / 5
The New Place / 6
Renting / 7
Three Bridges Building / 8
October, Commencement Bay / 9
Fall Gospels in Old Town / 10
Tacoma / 11
The Water in These Dried Things / 12
First Winter / 14
From This Angle / 15
Anniversary: Four Plus Change / 16
Understated Garden / 17
Apology after Saying I Have Been Married for
    One Hundred and Fifty Years / 18
Walk Me to the Moon / 19
Conversation Before June Solstice / 20
One Summer / 21
You See Yourself as You Might Be / 24
Incomplete Plan for the End of the Year / 25
Clown Curse / 26
Saturday in December Light / 28
The Mail, November / 29
The Birthday Ministry / 30
The List of People You Wanted to Be / 31
Non-League Play / 32
His Place at the Table / 33

Dishes / 34
There / 35
Kickspace / 36
Table / 37
Late August, Dog Days / 39
Horse Heaven Hills / 40
Old Town Pears / 42

II. AWAY

To Make Ends Meet / 45
The Silence After March / 47
One Kind Boy / 48
Eighth Grade Spring / 50
Petition for Sister Angela McCarthy / 51
Your People / 52
These Matters / 53
Your River, Your Morning / 54
What Stopped You for Years / 55
The Battery in October / 56
Driving North in Late September Rain / 57
March, Hawks Prairie / 58
Sleeping Till Noon / 59
In Mary Anne Waters' Book Jacket Photo / 60
Rescue / 61
The Here After / 62
To Stay Beyond the Season / 63
Poem for Flemming Palle Hansen, Danish Resistance / 64
The Grenå / 65
In the One / 66
Spider Said / 67
A Box of Spider's / 69

Even Better Than Luck / 71
Cate at the Kitchen Table / 72
Heir Apparent / 73
Jim Returns Wearing Picasso's Shirt / 74
At Clancy's Fruit Stand / 75
In the Wenatchee Valley Late March / 76
Wasps / 77
What Muriel Taught Jim and Jim Taught Me / 78
On Lunch Duty, the Principal Considers Intelligent Design / 79
The Hoop in Wallace Stevens' Backyard / 80
Custodians / 81
Voucher / 83
He Nails his Poems to the Cabin / 84

HOME

*You nearly have to be born
into a place to know what's
going on and what to do.*
　　　　　　　—John McGahern

Poem for Jonas Before Independence Day

The celebration begins tomorrow.
No one will settle for candles and cake.
Distance between us is metered in marks
where people have stepped out of their lives.
Melissa gave up a child and her apartment
over the store. Little things mean more
than they should. Starlings are in the fig trees.
People on 27th painted a brick house white.
A neighbor races up the alley
as if some god will mend any child struck.
Tomorrow they will hang the flags in Old Town.
Nothing frees my sleep of the man racing
after his bus. He waves one hand, his raincoat
no more help than the briefcase banging his knee.
The driver always sees him and continues.
No flag unfurls here. I snap clean the rug
that announces the bunker's entrance.
Today I practice my basement anthem. Its slow
deep refrain sounds best against concrete walls.
Nothing explodes or sparkles in this dark.
I keep safe a place for children, for the first lost dog.

Near Spring, Old Town

Tacoma, Washington

The famous neighbor pulls weeds
in her rockery like another mother

down the block whose peonies make
their quiet way underground this short month

when rain clouds loom as dark as loam
on the roughed hands of working women.

Work and worship, they genuflect
in the shadow of St. Patrick's tower.

Women praise this warm earth.
Their hands turn beds to borders

for lavender and alyssum to cross.
They make a place safe for snakes,

sparrows, a strip of color and shade.
One woman cannot see the other.

They have daughters not home from school,
jobs, mail on the counter, the idea of May.

One woman's pine tree casts a shadow
within feet of the other's yard, one has a row

of plum trees ready to line white light
for neighbors to follow to Commencement Bay.

Days from now when March clouds hail,
they will warm their hands with cups of tea.

What the Day Provides

Keep this morning safe in a pocket,
protect its slow light and the couple
walking at five-thirty, his hair white,
hers gray. Tilt it back like a miniature
pinball prize. Play over the couple walking
beneath the line of Japanese plum trees.
Stop them mid-hill where
their matching green sweatshirts
set off the burgundy leaves.
Freeze at the moment they turn
to the street and spot the white ball
rolling past them along the curb.
Advance it slightly to see them try to stop
its free flight down McCarver Street,
the woman's quick-foot miss,
to see them smile the smile of kids
trying to hold back the tide.
Nothing out this window answers it all—
the woman misses the ball over and over,
each time she's giddy with her try,
each time they look uphill to apologize.

The New Place

No wind moves the curtains in the brick house.
He has no other wives to remind him of the cabin.

His father was all weather maps, the gulls circling
beneath gray skies. The first north wind with clouds

meant snow. A father's *maybe* showed allegiance.
If morning became rain, no blame settled in the house.

Weather fails no one in the new place. The trace
of snow on the Olympics, light from night tugs

before Maury Island, the whistle of the early freight
to Portland live in the house with no ghosts.

He owes no one winter, morning starts and stays.
Today may be counting bells at the crossing gate,

starlings in fig trees, a neighbor girl's missed
shots pounding against the garage.

Once a woman he loved saved him a box of snakes.
When he opened the box, it was empty.

A man with such a gift knows the sound of skin
kept close, knows the twists in confined space.

She could have given him one field with enough snow
to keep hawks on the fence posts.

At the window in the brick house,
he hears his mother laugh over missing snakes.

She says she feels her bones disappear.
He sees the man who lied for snow drive a highway

and drift through winter longing for the woman
who caught fear. Books rest on new shelves.

Renting

The mail says enough on the envelopes.
The Post Office crosses out, tags,
forwards your old life to the new.
You love the sound of vanish,
the wash-like swish of a ring
down a drain or the sudden lift
of the sharp-shinned hawk disappearing
tail up over the laurel. Sparrow shadow
and feathers remain like ghosts
in the yard where your children played.
You tuck wishing in a pocket with prayer
like hidden cash you doubt you earned.
Days are made of small acts,
a five-mile walk to Lincoln Hardware
for a parlor broom like your mother's
with four rows of stitching, a wood handle
thick enough to swing at bats.
You march home like a kitchen soldier,
broom and Mt. Rainier over your right shoulder.

Three Bridges Building

Give me a building
with the right name,
a wooden storefront
with an apartment upstairs,
gold leaf letters on glass
over the entry door
understated, like a scarf
perfectly tied.

I leave you a note:
Meet at Three Bridges Building.
The single concrete bridge
will keep us counting ways
over the gully where stolen bicycles
and city deer lie in silence.

We will rendezvous
like pals after paper routes,
measure time by daylight,
by what we do and when it's done.
No one will be late.
First to arrive waits at the rail
to watch the gully trail twist
through blackberry and alder
descending three miles north
to Old Town and sea level.

October, Commencement Bay

Yesterday, along the shore,
I thought of you, thought this
sun through fog, this light
at the beginning of the tunnel
turned the image on its head,
and then the freight train
to California passed,
and the hole in the fog lost
its ties to a path through stone—
it no longer meant through.
You would have seen this before,
Northwest fall, early morning
near water, waiting for the mountain
to reappear. Still, I wanted to show
it to someone, like I want the walkers
to see the rusty selves the leaves
leave after the first rain,
like I want everyone to hear
Fred Neil sing "Faretheewell."
The part of me pushing to say *listen*,
to tell, worries it should be enough
to know, to bow my head in praise
of the opening in sky, the way
day's start brings you to mind
and I have to tell no one
how I hold you here.

Fall Gospels in Old Town

Sunday's lesson was forgiveness, seventy times seven.
The gospel makes a stream of numbers,
this pew is another bench, all these sevens form
a time-lapse Mantle in pinstripes racing to first,
running away from the point, forgiveness.

Last night someone sneaked into the park, took baseball bats
to the statues in Never Never Land. Lumps of plaster faces
stare from the soft ground. An inside-out swing drove
Snow White's head to right, a slip of her black bangs lies
beneath a broken toadstool, night shade.

Never never, seventy times seven strikes at solid targets.
The freight trains to Portland make a fast read of tags,
each stroke and curve a letter no one answers.
A kid near here dresses in blackface for a class photo.
Multiply his bad joke by any number of trees, night sheets.

Margaret Ann trims a block of irises—fall's a fact.
Wilt Chamberlain's death leaves us to reconsider how we name
what we do not understand. What never shatters strikes
us as permanent. It takes a legendary kiss to wake
the unforgiving, a man to rethink Goliath.

Tacoma

Cities are times of day
James Wright

The cooler at JJ's Pizza by the Slice
is a square moon across 21st.
The radio voice is a friend, security,
someone to choose your music.
Your stack of fiction is a fortress.
Atwood stares from the jacket,
faces down the room.
The wind rattles the mail slot with missives.
Even if night mail is wind,
you know what it spells.
These spells return like unstamped bills
you hoped would pay for one night's sleep.
The paperboys have an hour before work.
You know the drill after four—the first bus
follows the whistle for the late train to Portland.
Early customers at Wow's Etc. sit at the bar.

The Water in These Dried Things

. . . Our unfenced country
Is bog that keeps crusting
Between the sights of the sun.
                    Seamus Heaney

In the next room my wife talks to our grown son.
They say we need to clean death from our houses.
Those dried flowers on the mantel, the peonies
whose brittle burgundy I watched double in the mirror,
the hydrangea its papery snow flakes rigid enough
to break, the leather artichoke in the kitchen
I traded Neal for a book—all are in danger.

They have been at their books again, and I think
of the brick of turf from George Moran's shed
near Drumgildra, the brick drying on this desk
for ten years. It was thick with rain from the eighties
when Molly Moran sat across from me
over double shots of Powers holding a photograph
of my mother dead then fifteen years.

Too much the bog man here in this other room,
too willing to keep, to hold what's gone one way
to make it stay another, to keep her voice
with its lushness soft and steady as windless rain,
the silent falling strings earth to sky
in layers whose refrains are the kind things
someone whispers when I have lost, when

my understanding matches the dog's sleeping
at my side. Words are tone, and her tone
tells me *good dog, good dog, stay, stay.*
I think to tell them the corkscrew willow in the vase
by the window smells of fresh water even now.
It is the Yakima River where it bends at the trestle,
the river my father swam after picking apples.

First Winter

Lynden, Washington 1971

Northerlies played tricks that season.
An early silver thaw made Waterford
of town, Christian School's chain link fence
shimmered crosshatched diamonds,
raspberry vines were glass baskets
strung to cool, a mountain of corn
glistened in the feed store parking lot
one morning before silage.
A cloud marked Fishtrap Creek
snaked its way toward the berry ranches.
When Van Slyk delivered heating oil,
his Clydesdales' harness bells rang cheer.
Beer chilled in the grocery outside of town,
and the lounges with drink had no dancing.
Churches owned corners, Reformed This and That—
people gave a teacher hell for assigning Kesey.
December, the landlord forgave the rent,
snow drifted at the east side of the house,
and a young wife walked a mile to work.

From This Angle

I say Sonny Liston, she hears sunny disposition.
She lives in night. I walk the dark of morning.
Our silences bump into each other.

One cloud through another is mist.
Her Mozart lingers beneath Coltrane.
She tells me of Theresa of Avila, her heart in glass.

At my desk Roberto Clemente wears Pirate black.
He stays in the air, his plane forever ascending.
Our icons are sovereign flags.

We fall to each other in isosceles dependence,
our baseline weighted with accidents and opposites,
saints and complaints. She hates crowd noise on TV.

I think the way in is the suicide squeeze, the way out
a fast ball behind the head. No instinct tells us lean in.
The finger meant to type *trace* makes *grace*.

Crows' racket calls the eye, these black dots
an ellipsis to the red tail atop the neighbor's pine.
Some wrong numbers last a lifetime.

The photo I think is my daughter turns
into her mother fourteen years before the knock
at my door. Sneakers in the dryer are kettle drums,

and Allie is every lost love whose allegiance
we long to keep. What could be better, this game
and all our favorite lines on the inside of our mitts.

Anniversary: Four Plus Change

I have loved you in dog years,
followed you through dog-eared pages
of fiction, hesitated where I imagined
you stopped. I wonder if the line
where the field out the window
turns to flame is where you drifted
from the page, and if in pausing, you saw
the stable in France and us at the window
when lightning struck the pasture.
You spent the night on the hall floor
propped like a woman reading in bed.
You hated the horses kicking the stalls.
We talked through the night until fear lay
on its side like a shoe blown apart.

Understated Garden

She bags the black spot
like one packs apple slices
for school snacks.
He rakes willow and pear leaves
into a single pile, each stroke
a rustle to shush the crime
scene near the rose. She wears
gloves, secures evidence
in plastic sacks. He shakes
his head, spies a clothespin
he's dragged in the heap.
He considers stooping
to cull this wood and wire,
hopes he will find it again
when he scoops them into the bin.
She turns to the rosemary,
unsheathes her herb shears,
snips the blue-flecked sprigs
winding over chives and sage,
tosses them near his feet.
He wants to say cut
that spindly bay leaf,
take it to the ground.
Though she favors it
above all others, its green
cure-all leaves him counting
an impossible number
of soups and stews necessary
to keep things on the level.

Apology after Saying I Have Been Married for One Hundred and Fifty Years

At six a.m. the neighbor's dogs
bark, and I wake, knowing
the call, a bit of dog myself
after a line thrown for a laugh
sticks crossways with a woman
given to forgiveness. A stand-up
man keeps some things sacred,
though laughter has long legs,
wears diaphanous silk, and clicks
like spiked heels. I heel as well
as most, though when she grabs the ear
and twists, I stop typing altogether.
Some lessons come with practice.
I stop digging up the line,
You remind me of your mother.
I stay in the garage for cover,
and after hours of quiet, I surface,
gun-shy about this offer:
With dog division it appears
we have been married 34.25 years.

Walk Me to the Moon

Where Old Town starts,
a hundred-pound salmon
floats like a weather vane
five feet off the ground.
It heads in full sequin splendor
toward the Olympics, tail flashing
the tide flats and Rainier's outline
in dark she says will soon be moon.
The Welcome Clock stands green,
its face white enough for time.
Tonight rounds out August, a quiet
too quiet for Saturday on this block
of restaurants and bars. Sidewalk diners
at Café Divino lean in to one another.
Night talk is secrets and whispers.
This one evening she pulls me from fiction.
We walk to the bay, stand shoulder to shoulder
with the clock, watch the eastern sky
for the promise she knows will return
like a man with a face full of words
he no longer knows how to say.

Conversation Before June Solstice

For a minute, my right eye
is blind as I stand and rewind
the film on the Sixties, the end
of a decade I try to explain
to these sophomores.
I want to call you to ask
if this is something I should fear
approaching my seventh decade.
Of course I see the asphalt
in North Dakota where he fell—
like a bag of rocks, I'd say,
if he weren't my father, if he
hadn't carried me so many nights
with the whooping cough,
ear aches, comforted me
after sirens set off bad dreams.
Last night I shined my weejuns
with Kiwi paste, spit-shined
them the way he taught me,
heard him say shabby shoes
ruin the best suit.
The touch that never fades
is his arms over my shoulders
teaching me the full Windsor,
standing on his tiptoes
to see over me to the mirror.
Last night, you said,
I want to die fast like your father.
I said, I don't like to think
about shit like that.

One Summer

He carried a bag of starlings.
Their round impressions thumped
the sides of burlap like a child's
quick kicks in a blanket fort.
The squealing stopped when he rested,
their stillness a short nap. Awake,
he saw rats masquerading as shore birds.

One summer he lived in a chair.
The world was a window facing north.
The framed sky was day.
Consider Monday the third week of June.
One cloud filled the square in a gray wash.
Gulls crossing glass were ideas quickly forgotten.
Crows started as names of people to call
then smeared across a page.
When a day fit into a box he faced, voices
behind his head were sounds without vowels.

Before the chair, he carried the sack.
It was penance and ticked like a bomb.
Everyone would hear the clicking beaks.
He cinched the top tighter,
and when he shifted hands, he hid
so no one would be near
if a cramp or a slip caused the bag to drop.
Some days his hands were no good.
He went places he would not have to explain.

Back in the chair,
numbers 1–20 ran down the glass page,
each number and a period
the size of a starling's eye and then sky.
He had to make a list of guests for the wedding.

His fingers would not hold the pen.
His wife's sentences were subtitles
running across the glass like a news ticker.

He found himself empty-handed, outside.
In traffic he fidgeted at stoplights.
His head was that pie,
four-and-twenty black birds pressed
the crust of his skull to get to sky.
If all the feathers flew, the picture
from the chair would be his weather
after he drove the empty head home.

When he forced himself to move,
he was beside himself,
a time-lapsed figure leaving the chair.
He was those lights in the poster *Paris at Night*,
a trail of himself traveling light,
no connection between feet and floor,
hand and door. He felt nothing
unless he had to speak.
He had no answers—say *Paper or Plastic?*
Words were jumbled sticks
in the bottom of a sack.

Currency. He wanted to reach deep
into a bag of words to find an answer.
Questions came with answers.
He was unnecessarily placed in the middle.
If they wanted him to play, he would play.
He would let them win. The clerk in Colmar
knew the price of bread and wine.

She picked what she needed from his palm,
smiled. He nodded, breathed, *Merci*,
its sound so close to what it was.
When his wife asked for the list,
his palm to the sky said it all.
He was not Francis.
He wanted no birds to alight.
Even a man who lives in a chair knows
he is real in the way a lamp stands in a room.

You See Yourself as You Might Be

and when you wake, you sigh,
    fade back to the weightless moment
without giving yourself fully to sleep,
    knowing what you committed
in dream was dream, and the path
    to hide or disappear, the way to face
disgrace or scorn could be left
    for another time, for some other
stunned by remorse, leaning to over-
    turn what should have never come
to pass, and for days you remember
    your wickedness undone,
the dreamy glide as your act unravels
    and you march a few steps in place
parading all your goodness, your
    grace has been restored, sleep has taken
all that you had, and now you think
    you have it back and more, more
the saint, more the righteous, when really
    what you could have done
rides the night waiting for you to rest.

Incomplete Plan for the End of the Year

Simmer without boiling,
favor stock over broth, count
minutes after solstice twice,
cool long enough to clear
window steam, repeat until birds
no longer appear at the feeder.
Trust the slot not the spoon,
strain with cheesecloth,
sprinkle in pepper and thyme,
hum "The Tennessee Waltz"
like your mother making beds,
mix baking powder biscuits,
cut them with a juice glass,
wait for each thin moon to rise
and float like the big man dances
with grace enough for two.
Fold cloth napkins into mitres,
set six places like popes facing.
Stand red dogwood twigs
in the vase with water,
center between beeswax candles.
Wait for the second ring at the door,
answer without speaking, show
no surprise when the first person
to arrive fails to know your name.
Consider each guest unanswered mail.
Names matter less late in December.

Clown Curse

A man in darkness puts on the red nose,
slaps his hands like a seal and says *fish, fish*.

This black suit and flippers never hide the eyes.
Who believes this string of silk scarves is all one

when it unravels from a wet suit pocket?
They demand tuxedoes, white gloves and blood.

They want Michael Jackson's old nose
back on his beige face. They want real knives,

women spinning slightly behind schedule.
When he practices in the tank, his wife says

Too many bubbles, more locks & chains,
don't muddy the water, don't surface too soon.

Once man starts to spin the plates, pause is wreckage.
One missed touch and the wobbling starts.

He's bound to remember everyone's card.
The rabbits must have pink ears and coats

like harmless clouds. Some days, standing
on the ball takes all his attention.

Falling is no way out. If he touches ground,
he will wear the big shoes, the polka dot suit,

drive the tiny car in circles for the children
who open and close hundreds of hands

until he honks the bulbous horn again
and again. He sleeps the sleep of a man

with the quivering leg. He leaves juggled fish
in the air, and what he holds must fly.

Even air demands its fill. He's hoarse
from all the barking. If he finds his voice,

he swears, this time he'll draw the line
at fiery hoops & poodles marching on hind legs.

Saturday in December Light

Carry me into this day,
hold me against all fear,
hum for me a melody to wind
this wind into three-part
harmony, layer one voice
over the other.

Watch with me this Merlin
darker than day, whisper
for me a warning through willow,
to black cap, sparrow, and wren.
Keep for me secrets I speak,
impractical prayer for raptor and prey.

Plait for me a sleep cross-hatched
with faces—mother filters through child.
Eyes over years recur the way
a sister's hand makes the same letters
her mother turned a fluid blue
strand across the card I save.

Wait with me in this thin between
when first and last light mingle,
lovers whether left or leaving.
Draw for me the names in window steam,
his choice for girl, hers for boy.
Learn by heart the shapes they make.

The Mail, November
for Loren Sundlee

My friend from Minnesota owns the snow.
When he writes, it swirls in silk veils
thin enough to bring desire home
to this house where the rain slicker

lies in the corner near muddy boots.
Winter, he says, brings its light.
The letter's crisp and dry in my hands.
His lines show new ice on the pond,

a stand of sugar maple, his father's barn.
He's finished one round of chores
before sitting with his wife over coffee.
Even on paper, their stove pops its clean heat.

What he sets in air there whispers here,
finds us awash in record rains.
I read aloud his line about their horse, lost,
the unannounced neighbor who delivers a colt

for their daughter to work this winter.
From the den, Cam says, Amazing.
Our neighbor's dogs bark at us for an hour
as we channel their runoff past our house.

For thanks, I offer gray, say, We lost the islands
days ago, gravity works given a proper ditch.
At the shore, one crabapple won't let go—
it's all balled up for December and curious seals.

The Birthday Ministry
for many, this will be their only card

Forgive this card—
these snaking streamers,
the pointed hats,
candles with tear-drop
flames, the tired refrain
the traditional-wishes-team
clicked from their pull-down
menu of blessings woven
neatly around the tail
of their clip-art mouse.

Pray any card calls back
your mother's trick
to turn one day
into a searchlight stopped.
In the halo at the table
you are six, her voice wraps
around you like a satin ribbon,
you wear the tee shirt
with multi-colored stripes,
if you sit at the chair edge,
your feet reach the floor.

Today the shaft of light
is your name highlighted
on my list, your birth year
cupped in parentheses.
You are this Thursday
in my year of Thursdays.
May the grace of this blessing
keep you strong years past
the smudge of smoky wishes
as I keep secret your gift to me.

The List of People You Wanted to Be

makes each slow day no one calls
a quiet to lie in like a hot bath.

Some days the simple nothingness
of your life is deep heat for the ache

envy worked into the muscle and tendon
you thought should be somebody.

The nobody you've begun to love
is calm in the halfway wisdom

common brings. The names you held
make a dream you drape in sparkling

ribbon, its shimmer all surface,
its hollow a barrel to echo laughter

at your naked want. Your list is a vest.
Those you've outgrown, snake out the fob

slinking to find a face fit for applause.
You find favor in failure. Fallen gods

make worship less than wishing. You flash
a gap-toothed grin at fame's mirage.

Faults are the path worn in stone steps.
You map veins trailing across your cheek,

follow the lines through your day, find
the way of a grandfather come to visit.

Non-League Play
for Seamus and Liam

The skaters at Garfield Park favor
the bench near the cannon.
They are shooting stars grinding
chrome tails across the green metal seat.
Boys with no taste for Little League
or soccer play follow the leader
on the Wright Academy tennis courts.
They hang the helmets mothers demand
on net standards as they pump and glide,
segments of a stretching snake
winding in and out of bounds.
No one calls anyone about playing time.

On the infield, three girls work a golden
retriever in an equilateral romp for a Frisbee.
He wears a scarf bib and tosses
his head on the way to return the disk.
The girl near second and heading to right
makes an over the shoulder grab,
her grace a silent Say-Hey ballet.

Hackeysackers slacking in cottonwood shade
mime bicycle riding in quick kicking spurts
as they keep what is soft aloft. A new kid arrives,
the circle widens. No timeouts, no coaches
to make ceremony or ritual of substitutions.
Everybody plays as long as he likes.

The grandfather near the slides
watches his grandson run away
from the play toys heading for the dog.
Midway, the boy stomps white clover.
He changes direction, chases bees, on his way-
ward path through these minor leagues.

His Place at the Table

Hollis worries the yarn,
a stitch for her, a stitch for him,

a blend of colors twined together.
Her sleight of hand feathers gray

through heather as she rocks
and stares into the fire, pattern

kept in wool to pull over the ears
of a grandson carrying cordwood.

Hats line the mantel, across them
elk follow bear follow snowflake.

She is slow motion before the fire
surrounded by the rhythmic creak

of wood on wood, the tick of needles,
the pop of pitch, the push of heat.

In the mudroom, a mackinaw hangs
on the same peg all winter. The boy backs-in

a load of alder. Bacon and biscuits drift
toward the door he kicks shut.

Hollis calls breakfast, pours coffee,
sets two places facing. The boy sloughs

jacket, gloves. Sits. She snatches
his hat, touches a hand to his cheek.

Her one-word call is all that passes there,
this quiet, wood-smoke settling on wool.

Dishes

Mornings while she sleeps
he empties the sink, fills it
with soap and hot water,
starts coffee, washes
dinner plates and glasses,
soaks the silverware
in the rice pan, each move
amplified as if all the house
leans to the sound of forks
set on a plate, a cupboard
closing. This day, he finds
a new sponge near the faucet,
and as he scrubs pesto from a bowl,
he thinks of the President,
and though he has no envy,
he wonders when the last time
he knew dishwater up to his wrists,
felt the inside edge of a bowl
come clean in his hands.

There

Every table has its place whether set
or let alone where the long gone
or gone wrong appear. There,
you say, nodding to a chair,
the spot near the window.
The cough of one who remains
dares to start a story in the full circle
of Sunday dinner with traces
of the missing—Father's plane crash
tale took off over the beef,
his carving knife waving mid-air
like a one-winged Auster; a brother
reaches for it from the high chair,
the flight path always toward Mother
and the return, this time in sudden fog,
stutters over the center, father unable
to find the road he used to navigate.
With or without the house, the room,
the furniture, these reappear—
the taste of warm biscuits buttered,
a sputtering engine and possible fence posts
out the plane window where your sister's
mashed potatoes remain untouched.

Kickspace

You haunt the edge of the day,
walk the dark hall before the paper
when raccoons wake back-porch dogs,
when the wind tricks motion lights
and steals the dark. Your lover sleeps
in her place next to impressions you made.
Over time you open doors like a man
cracking safes, you avoid the third stair,
you neither cough nor sneeze.
In deference to spiders and mice,
you ease each step in a soft kiss
like wool on ice. You usher them
to kickspace for an escape at daylight,
a way to disappear in the waking world.

Table

Just to say the word
home, *that one word alone,*
so pleasantly cool.
Issa

Your hand waves over the table,
the index finger makes its mark
as if to push a strip of sand mandala
to water, each color a street
you crossed home and away,
patterns a maze, ingrained numbers
tumble and click as quick
as addresses known by heart.
Sidewalks stall at corners,
curbs give pause when the traffic
of your past races Dublin-fashion,
surprise-right, you years looking left.

Blueberry scones you knead
mean nothing to your skin
until tucking in the fruit brings back
the griddle, bananas and berries
you dropped in pancakes Saturdays
for children kneeling on chairs.
In his last year, your father could recite
the names and numbers of every place
he lived even if he could not find his keys.

Kitchen tables in houses housing others
slip like sand to water. Voices surface
in a mix of places where the missing
return for those able to hear, and story
keeps the rooms near enough to taste garlic

stuffed in a Sunday roast. Red wine swirls
with an uncle's toast. Your sister
in white laughs your mother's laugh.
Your grandson sits in your father's chair.
The child's full face keeps them layered
one over the other, there.

Late August, Dog Days

I have plans for a dozen dogs,
winter fires, rain storms, and pock-
marked rivers as quiet as November
with the world off to work.
One dog first, maybe a year
to find its place near the back door,
in the truck, a year for us to settle
into a name it can wear and I can hear
whispered as the coffee drips
in the dark. Plans call for cold weather,
for books mapping a course
in various corners of the house.
When daylight is more answer
than question, we walk an hour out,
an hour back. Pace means nothing
with a dog and a day. On the way out,
I'll chant the names of those away.
The way back, I'll list what they left
and assign it to the living.
Afternoon winks its way to dark,
a whiskey neat and a letter,
a few lines to know by heart,
a walk for the mail. One day
closer to the second dog.

Horse Heaven Hills

She makes sense of the kettle's whistle,
holds a thin hand high, *No one move.*
Silence steeps these rooms.

One day we will have waited
long enough. We will not bother
to ask, to answer, to speak.

We will know more than we imagined,
less than these poplars lined at attention.
Wind rattles windows, dust presses glass,

storms sift through cracks no one sees.
Sweeping days we stoop, branch
and shadow, broom meets pan.

We side-step the worn places people passed.
Tumbleweed ticks across the porch rolling
toward the river. Three chairs face three windows,

books stack in uneven piles. Paper slips mark places
like buckets for roof leaks in a place rain forgot.
Cars passing are clouds to the west. They crush

gravel into a stream of edges droning
until the drop to the river swallows sound.
The horizon's a thick chalk line across flat earth.

She counts time in a bead's descent.
Midday iced tea sweats clear lines over amber.
A letter balances near her knee, the cursive

breezes left to right, its drift a soothing run
in the thick heat. Her fingers smooth the folds,
naps and paragraphs, paper and ink.

Evening she walks the dogs through the tree line.
The shadows close around her, a cool windfall,
the rustle of leaves polite applause.

Old Town Pears

Immature pears lined the cedar fence
one tear of rust for each day of the week
like seven hard ideas to last past
this moment, like hand-written letters
unconnected, reconsidered, thin at the top,
balanced in thick-bottomed charm
never to be bigger than this moment
when the sun shows their freckled faces
dumb in afternoon light, silent forever
in their sameness blushing quietly
this series of cursive Ss all capital and leaning
the way penmanship practice made patterns
with no sound and letters never meant to be words
held their place adding up to nothing.

AWAY

. . . No easier this being
good in worlds away from home . . .
— Robert Huff

To Make Ends Meet

Near the ruined gate bound
with rope and wire, the wood's
weariness holds the shaggy pony
like a plea to settle.
The stone fence in the rough pasture
stops for this intersection. The leafless
scrub on its other side leans in a scramble
of sharp sticks sprinkled with berries.

When she walks here, she stops
with a pocketful of apple, her song
for the pony part chant, part cooing,
hand and apple to muzzle,
one hand to ruffle its scruffy mane.
She stops here missing Liam, stops
missing when its breath warms her hand,
when its turn turns to nuzzle.

Once her mother handed her a cup
and saucer so thin they settled in her hand
like a moth any wind might whisk away.
In the cup a dried spear thistle peeked
over the lip brittle and sharp as if her
first sip were steeped in prickly bracts
she needed to soothe with the cooling
whistle of her breath blown so.

She tells no one her fear of falling,
wants no one to know she's weightless,
walks in day the dream others have—
tumbling and no means to break their descent.

Once Liam asked why she watched her shadow
when she jumped, why she chased
the tufts of dandelions to make more wind.
She tried to answer, *Flying is not falling.*

Shadows are tethers and ponies glide
only ten hands above solid ground.
Her mother knows. She gathers
things from her garden to fasten
the child, to help her with so much air.

The Silence After March

for Megan MacNichol

The night gives him up—
a prisoner crosses a border
to dumb stares and open arms.

Pear blossoms scatter like search lights
in a spring so cold, one goldfinch is god.
The reception line fills

with women waving willow branches.
The thin wands trail tender leaves
and ripple an arc of light.

He wears dark glasses, his hands unbound.
One woman imagines blue eyes,
another thinks blindness freed him.

No flags fly in this sanctuary. A boy hums
a song with words in someone else's language.
The swaying women's shoulders touch.

This wall of cotton winds a path to a garden.
No one speaks of release or conditions.
A freckled girl stands near a table.

She holds a bouquet of fortunes bunched
like a white hydrangea she cannot control.

One Kind Boy

Girls overlook the kind boys.
Something soft in their voices,
they are breakable boys
no one dislikes, no one fears.
Sharon runs into the room barefoot
and black-eyed. She puts her feet
on the chair of a boy so shy
his name makes him nervous.
She's safe here for an hour,
safe next to him.
He is the indefinite pronoun
on the other end of a phone
who listens and nods.

Some boys are calm water,
clean sheets, chimney smoke
straight to the sky.
They are expected weather.
Nothing in them stops breathing.
Girls tell them bitter secrets
of older boys who switch a fast blade
of anger with one scowl.

The girls' trust spurns an edgy lust,
turns a few boys from themselves
when they find they must hold
secrets like a bowl filled
with someone else's excitement.

They refuse to be brimmed with danger
girls know they will never possess.
Possession has power as dark and deep
as black leather, and no one mentions
the soft cushion of its feel. It becomes
background for razor sharp studs,
the jangle of buckle and shine.

The boy who turns from himself
knows leather softens a fall.
He remembers all the Sharons
sitting near him, safe with his quiet,
sure he will be there when a sudden wind
makes them shudder, when betrayal
leaves them leaning to the part of him
he's worked to scar with cuts of his own.

Eighth Grade Spring

One son falling is no end,
salvation swings both ways.
The crucifix crosses
nuns in motion.
Sister heads west,
and Jesus, like clock-work,
heads east, his tiny chrome feet
soldered one over the other.
His hands point to sky and earth
ready to cartwheel for us all,
his station airy in its tumbling
before black habit crossing
playground or classroom.
Sister O's swinging for fences,
snapping rulers, correcting tenses.
No mistake's mortal
until spring sun pushes freckles
across the low throat of one girl.
Pray for skin's perfect patterned falling.
Give forgiveness a place to stay.

Petition for Sister Angela McCarthy

Neither the buds on the Japanese plum
nor the bald eagle on the pilings
behind the closed fish market,
not the end of the rains, not
sun on this holiday weekend
manifest God. Though something
knocks besides the radiators, nothing
dramatic like a cheese toast Madonna,
nothing desperate like a sick child,
this woman, an *old woman* in her words,
a nun who spends her day
with scripture. After the chaos
of classrooms, reluctant students,
and cranky parish priests,
this woman is today's God-call.
She praises her gift of time,
the quiet for reflection, appreciates
her place in a timber town for decades
the image of the sorrowful mysteries.
This is more wish than prayer, more hope
than conversion, for the sake of those
least likely to claim righteousness, grant
a Hereafter beatific and fair in the way
the car passing on the right reappears
miles ahead in those blessed blue lights.

Your People

Jefferson, Oregon

Gather each hint of highway and mint,
the open fields and pasture creeks,
fences keeping acres of thick grass
here from thick grass there, and summer
sun off the back porch, the early heat.
Hold them like the walk into town.

Keep the town for your own, borrow
the sound of your father's voice calling
to a friend, hear it echo his father, timbre
firm in your throat, the way one uncle's eyes
show the sly humor of a cousin
close enough to be a brother.

Even if you had a stomach for the city,
if parking spaces and trolley sparks
in the windows of closed shops
meant stars, the barber who cut hair
for all the men with your name
waits with the razor and strop.

The first death calls you home.
Farewell is a long song best sung
with feet icing in a pasture creek,
redwing blackbirds on fence posts,
the melody of shop-door bells ringing
over thresholds worn by your people.

These Matters

He leans closer to hear the small whisperings . . .
                                        Raymond Carver

What's left is your day—
fountain pen, loose change, his ring
of keys bunched in your hand
the way your hand once fit in his.
In the closet, his ties drape in silky silence.
They are as far from shirts as the dead
from work. You slept so many hours
when his motion in the dark gathered
what he carried into another morning.

You wear mourning for weeks
convinced the sum of this change fits
a breast pocket, its pulse a clockwork
ticking in accord with your heart
until it stops, and the smooth stride
of two in step falters and pitches
you off balance, his whisper missing,
your pace broken. You worry his beret
between thumb and finger, inch the fabric

of its band round, a felt circle turning.
And the talk of tomorrow, deer at first light
look back as dumb as unopened mail.
The raccoons fear less each season.
The woman you love has bolts of wood
waiting. She sees what sleeps until her turn
frees a shape she learned from a tree.
What you have made of words makes you
lean at this quiet, the stilled voice pressed
in thick paper, letters set before ink.

Your River, Your Morning

River runs close, thin skin
we see through again carries
what's fallen further away slipping
toward the bend where tamarack
torch the hillside as descent
hints where white water stutters
and splits past the rock shaped
like a bear's back facing west,
and the Yakima leans toward
Yakima with a brief tease to Selah,
ever the step-sister, overlooking
the river headed off on its own
passing town for city soon given
to sage and cottonwood shade falling
over backwater ponds circled
with cattails and lines
redwings fly fifty feet below
the stick baskets osprey build
near the bend before Sunnyside
where pelicans fill the eddy
like nuns in the habit of bathing,
their white on water a cumulous sky.
Down is up downriver
near the place your father built
a neighborhood of houses so close
to the same water you watch
ease past your morning miles
upriver, years to the sea.

What Stopped You for Years

Nor is one silence equal to another
Donald Justice

What kept you from talking to the woman
at the market is a fence down. You wake
and high grass covers post holes,
tree lines fail to mark where things stop and start.
Kelly serves your coffee. You address her this once
by name. Even *Good morning* wants a story.
You tell her the title of a book you wish you read
at twenty-three. The man in the tweed cap
and windbreaker sits across from you for three years.
Every morning the two of you keep within your news.
Today, he speaks, something about Boston's late run,
and you mention Carlton Fisk. He turns half around
at this and says Buckner deserved so much better.
He reminds you of Justice with those big glasses,
and you walk into your day recalling another man's
work and worth. You drive toward Ahtanum Ridge.
Three songs on the radio and you know someone
chooses their order—it's like listening to a line drawing,
the pen never lifts until black makes sense of white.
This morning has nothing to do with things given up.
You know five songs that could be next.

The Battery in October

When we conference on the mound,
this left-hander tells me Jane Gallagher
grew up and became Nancy Griffith.
I'm here to talk placement, thinking fastballs
out of the strike zone and off-speed
stuff, starting out and staying out.
We are too old for heat, too tired
for power after power.
Our game knows no lucky strikes.
The speeds we change may be misnamed.
Nothing means as much as finding Jane.

Each year the season runs closer to winter.
Strong hitters look nothing like Killibrew.
The heart of the order is so young. We still
push it in close to set up away, and we
know all the weaknesses worth knowing.
Before I return behind the plate, I mention
the woman who translates Fujii Yoshiyasu.
Lefty recites
When the gate of my house is open,
you can see a green mountain.
If you don't mind being lonely,
you are welcome anytime.

No one hurries us.
Jane's in Austin.
We've got two outs,
the wind's blowing in from right.

Driving North in Late September Rain

Her passing occasions cleaning gutters,
preparations for the sacrament of winter.
This college girl in the fast lane drives
toward Canada with everything she owns.
A laundry basket holds a quilt, coats fill
side windows, chair legs pinion the dome light.
Sight-line northwest, a straw sunhat lies
near the back window two months before first frost.

Envy fades to a dog gone—this scratching
only youthful pranksters ringing and running.
Cigarette memories no longer return
without the pain in the chest. New love's race
in the blood sleeps with someone else's hurt.
Summer follows her like a warrantee.

March, Hawks Prairie

First light on Hawks Prairie, an owl draws a flat line
into a stand of fir. Twin barns reappear on the Delta.

What returns without bidding is as sure as brothers
home to help with heavy chores, and more.

The slip to day catches night flight, paths cross,
chance lifts a curtain and certain structure

rises before dawn's stall keeps the hunter aloft.
Left to the morning, harriers will etch shadow marks

over marsh and sloped roofs. Rainier will float like a white
kite tethered to the river strung east through alder.

Songbirds are a month away. Last season
the path to the reach gave up the fanned wing

of a barn owl, one morning-after memento
dusting airy repose from the great horned dark.

Sleeping Till Noon

A morning missed is a woman
sitting across the aisle on the bus
to work every day for a year.
Miles of opportunities run
through his mind as he counts
days he never stopped to talk,
her auburn hair most certainly
gray by now, her green eyes
still looking out windows
in places he never imagined,
her life complete with no hint
of him even now rising at noon.

In Mary Ann Waters' Book Jacket Photo

she's in the driver's seat checking left,
her elbow rests out the window,
right wrist draping the wheel
as if she points to mileage.
When she speaks, the hand turns
on the word, a finishing stroke
to extend the line, draw sound
in a stream of ink on air.
This black and white plays her
like an old movie. Each projector click
calls for the trick to remake the end.
Nothing remains of her voice—she keeps
her edge in the eye, the iris glints,
the brow rises, fierce questions
and the fixed-stare wait for answers.
Evenings at the Uptown for beers,
she squints, waves away our smoke,
tender in her disgust. Some nights
she locks on a spot in the distance,
a screen door slams and something
she loves disappears in the heat.
Young, dumb enough to imagine,
each of us plans to drive her out of his life.

Rescue

The woman lost overnight
    in the Cascades falls
upon luck, the brief parting
    of clouds after days of snow,
her charmed moment nothing
    compared to the yellow flag
she finds to wave when the copter appears.
    She happens upon rain pants
abandoned in the evergreen dark,
    unbelievable and bright as summer
this November with record rains.
    The firs keep secrets in the understorey.
Seasons end and give up only color,
    a warmer dark, save rare occasions
when summer dogs after ground squirrels
    uncover in the underwood the grim
chronicles the Northwest tries to wash away.
    Still, no one carried her there.
She strapped on the shoes to wander
    where so many others were dumped
like unwanted papers from a boy who failed
    to be about his route. Some nights
the news turns otherwise, we see
    a rescue, a chopper ticks
from treetops' peril, lowers
    the basket to remove a woman whole,
alive, safe from the footage of so many
    others where ten men in rain
slickers stand looking at the ground,
    when it was bags not baskets.
And as the camera from a TV copter
    pulls back, we see a sort of sunny
corpse mark the spot as if someone
    willed a foul weather offering
so we might have our women back.

The Here After

One car, one road,
lost night, fog knows
shadow the way the leaf
touches shade. Someone
looks another direction,
the highway forgives
most of the time.
Those left use up
each other's luck,
fritter away chance
driving the numbers
with our windows open
radios howling,
navigating by the moon
whose white out-whites
years of crosses.

Our partings dress casually,
nonchalant. We want
the same look coming
and going, knowing
luck keeps us
five minutes longer for gas,
time for one hailstorm
to pass, or we freeze,
figure this is only a roll
if ice comes up,
those blown kisses,
unspoken misses turn
us to pillars. Still,
if we halt, we die.

To Stay Beyond the Season

Summer evenings in Ebeltoft,
two watchmen carrying lanterns
climb the courthouse steps
and sing the evening song.
Dumb tourists, we lean
against a timbered house.
Each window frames a vase
or something carved from stone.
Hollyhocks grow between cobbles
in the foot from curb to house.
We imagine winter gray,
walking streets free of tourists,
quiet save the occasional bicycle rattling
to the grocer or the road to Boeslum
where pastures fall to the sea.

The night men wear black hats
like miniature hatboxes with brims.
We follow in step back through town,
past the sweet shops and Kros,
their tables put up for the night.
Once they sing the town to sleep,
we are wide awake, worrying
about winter and the miles to walk
since they moved the library out of town.
In the book stacks, we will be spies
thumbing through texts for the one
or two words we know in Danish.
We pass the two aisles of books in English,
grab something on the move and ease
into the soft chairs to read until closing.

Poem for Fleming Palle Hansen, Danish Resistance

Slettestrand, Denmark

My morning at Slettestrand
offers an accidental beatitude.
The start is men and women
in wheelchairs, their attendants,
and a mat that runs to the sea.
As I cross their path,
I greet them in the Danish
I have, *God dag.*
A good day it is, this walk
to the shore, people wheeling
those unable to the ocean's edge
and bringing them back
for soup and cards, yards
from the German bunker
where a beach chair
is stationed on its roof.
Sand reclaims the concrete bluff
sixty years after the offensive.
The chair, too worn for occupation,
faces north, meek in its emptiness,
as the dunes inherit for all their worth.

The Grenå

Grenå, Denmark

I walked the creek before sun,
at midday, in the evening dark.
It ran through me as we moved
in this town unnoticed, steady,
heading to bigger water. In the year
without speech, I practiced
along the path where cyclists
with bike bells rattled their way
to the green grocers.

Swallows worked cattail stands
scattering feathers along the soft chine
of the rowboat wedged in the tussocks
of sedge. Locals draped longfish nets
like windsocks on fence posts,
their metal rings slack in all weather.
When Hanne taught me to say *å*,
my mouth shaped to whistle,
the opening small in the way
no *å* need grow to river.

Longfish got away in the translation.
Hanne deciphered through her
traditional meal. Circle the plate,
build a bone wheel with skeleton,
ceremony as rich as the fatty flesh
she told me was eel. I swallowed
their silence, the creek, the sea.

In the One

where they make you President,
your wife suggests the striped tie,
one brother writes a speech
to end the war. Your mother
thinks now you should apply
to Notre Dame. Pop wants a game
of catch in the Rose Garden.
Your sisters rearrange furniture,
take down all the flags.

Spider Said

We slept in the cottonwood, hid from school.
The river fog lingered, and we nestled in the soft crook
and slept until sun filtered through the high branches.

She climbed high after my boost.
Each step after my hands found the right place.
She was wind as she worked her way to the spot

over the back eddy. She said the osprey saw her
with its bank-side eye, marked her at this point
before she dove for streaks of silver.

She worried her hands in the fringe of her scarf,
twirled the wool with thin fingers and sang
River, river, take me home. Make me fish, make me stone.

After sun warmed the trunk, we walked to the trestle.
We called it recess. Most days the squatters had a fire.
Its smoke climbed the beams, split, rose over the tracks.

The trainmen called Spider and waved her to the fire.
She stood half behind me, half facing them.
Second Bridge carried the school buses.

They came for the small kids at noon. Lunch was apples,
hiding in the tower of empty bins, listening to the sorters
talk while they smoked behind the warehouse.

She liked the way the words and smoke reached us
together, said they rose like cartoon balloons.
I looked down on plastic hats and white coats, their arms

bent like swans as they talked. Spider said women
wished they could ride the river out of their lives,
said her mother taught her the river song at night

while she rubbed lotion into ruined hands. Spider said
this was not her river. When the big trucks hauled
the last apples, when frost covered cottonwood leaves,

her brother drove them west. She said, Some trees
are as good as grandfathers, trains are men's river,
school starts this way every year.

A Box of Spider's

Handmade Box
She turned it the way she played
a hard pack of Marlboros talking on the phone.
Each side told its story. A daughter folds
her mother's hand into squares,
a paper box, its sides covered
with her mother's faded cursive,
letters she longed to make perfect,
penmanship copied in notebooks.
She glazed pieces of notes and lists
into carefully cornered sections.
Her mother's capital *T*'s and *L*'s
slanted like skaters over pond ice.
Every letter linked to another, a string of ties.
Her aunt's script was so like her mother's,
she wondered if her mother
wrote to herself. On the top side,
a series starting *Please excuse,*
a portion of a note to school, Spider's full name,
its perfect upper case letters, capital C,
capital J, capital M. One for her mother,
one for her aunt, one her father left,
each the same cant, linked together
made someone the school wanted her to be.

What Lies Within
Cate knew the box's heart. She heard
the rattle a ring makes, gold ticking
into paper hardened over the years.
When she was Spider, her mother said,
*Everyone has a drawer they keep pieces
of days & places where lives steep.*

She knew her mother's drawer, the one
packed in the wooden box with gold
hinges each spring before they crossed
the mountains. Empty, it smelled
of Grandfather's cigars. Full, it ticked
and jingled with watches and bells, matches
with pictures of dancers, and swizzle sticks.
The box Spider made traveled within a box,
east to west, box to drawer.
Her mother carried it on her lap
as her brother drove. High school for Cate
was a day in literature class: Ma Joad burns
her stationery box before heading west.
Steinbeck's intersection of women lay in wait
for Cate to cross and carry out the other side.

The Names
What rattled, rang the sound of names
she read: *Catherine, Jane,* and *Moran.* Parts
of lives her mother wrote and rarely spoke.
Occasionally she called Spider *Cate.*
Sometimes *Jane.* She refused to utter *Moran.*
Mother reduced her father to a small noise
like a box with rock, walled him off,
kept him from the rest of the drawer.
Cate sang the names her mother excused,
three names for the girl late every fall,
gone every spring. Three names woven
in blue lines like ribbon strung by birds
looping faces and a place saved at the table.

Even Better Than Luck

Some days *even* crept into her sentences.
Cate hedged when speaking,
doubted when things worked.
She liked the faucet dripping,
her junk drawer that would not close.
With Jim, she thought, even,
even two years was a blessing.
Two years where a man made sense.
More is not enough if it requires luck.
She knew her mother's lines on this,
No man is luck, no time forever,
if he looks lucky, trade looks for clever.

Her dogs loved Jim's quiet step
in the garden, his voice at first light.
Cate's dogs said Stay, Jim, stay.
His words were votives in blue glass,
and when she spoke, he faced her
like a man staring into a fire.
Her mother taught her
to trust dogs before men.
Their first winter, he read Stevens'
poem about the snow man every night,
and when she questioned, he read
it again before they sat in the dark.
Even, she knew now, meant more
than in spite of, more than odds.
It was as sure as the poem.
Even the trees knew Jim had been
the nothing that is.

Cate at the Kitchen Table

As a girl, smudge pots were rusty uncles
to call when frost refused to leave.
Forbidden cisterns were secret silos

where she dropped wishing stones
like grain swallowed for safe keeping.
Men worked in water and smoke.

They clouded skies and refused to name
weather they feared. They spoke tenderly
of bees and dogs eating field mice.

Nothing this day made water of rain.
No southerly carried the protection
snow gave to the girl. A man's jacket

draped the chair Cate faced. She exhaled
a pall of smoke across table. She fought
as taught, the chill drink brought home.

Her wrist showed his blue mark left
beyond the twist and jerk when failed
words and fear conflated in force.

After the slammed door and spat gravel,
she tip-toed the chair with jacket, jawed
a smoke ring, topped their slow, dead fall.

Heir Apparent

The killdeer taught her more than her own
mother who made *child-of-the-failed-marriage*
the lead shoes she wore as a girl.

A mother herself, her list is wing-dip
and not some weight hammered from the slag
of blame. She spins circles to ward off strangers.

A scarf trails from a frightened gather of hair
like a kite tail. This mother's day starts marching
her daughter through the kitchen into the wind.

Waving arms lift them, and when the breeze
tricks water from their eyes, they whistle like wrens
and slip through green stems of salvia. This child

meets the air like a hummingbird. She hovers, darts,
then settles to lug water to pumpkins and sunflowers.
They hang the netting, and mother teaches daughter

to leave something for the crows. Two seeds and foil
rolled into a ring. Feed the heart and find the eye.
Keep nothing in your pockets. Travel light.

Jim Returns Wearing Picasso's Shirt

The sailor stripes make old men young.
His skinned head appears shades darker,
gray enough in black and white for tan.
Everyone has left him to me this time.
I hold him and kiss the top of his head.
Where his shoulders should be,
shirt folds into itself. He collapses
like a concertina, each fold tucked tightly
until he decreases to an idea. I cup my hands
to keep my parenthetical man from going out.
The shirt works its wonder—I carry him
to a bench above the bay and women stop to talk.
One knew him in Alaska, another
watched him from the bridge at Dakota Creek,
a silent boy bent on fish. When they start
with their questions, we disappear
like money and houses he lost on his own.
This visit he comes for me. I find him
in Picasso's white with blue period.
What I always meant to say falls in two
perfect sentences. He listens, nods, and I turn
him into a postcard I carry everywhere.

At Clancy's Fruit Stand

the big man himself pulls his knife
to cut a slice of golden delicious.
He says, This will change your life.
He's the eleventh of eleven,
knows work like some know prayer.
Clancy patched the wounded in Korea,
and when he came home,
drove his new Buick all over town.
Before his orchard, he hauled gold
from the Lovett Mine near Squilchuck.
These are no fool's gold. His eyes sparkle,
and he gives us one box free
to take to the coast for advertising.
We wave and he's singing Sinatra
in the shade of a red delicious tree.

In the Wenatchee Valley Late March

for Clarence Stumpf

smoke rises from mounds of prunings,
Kaolin clay covers the fruit trees
along the river as if some spider
blessed them in a gray glaze,
the orchards outlined as they wind
into the Cascades' green foothills.
It may snow again, then sun
will sift through this thin coat,
April days will push bud to the blossom
May wears like lace, and one man
lost seven years before the bees
whispers, a breeze in the rows
of young honey crisp his son tends.
It's too early for the one-man fruit stand,
too late to feel his thick, rough fingers
take your hand as if he understood the skin
of someone who works with words.

Wasps

Cocktails at the barbecue,
the host delivers the drinks,
wears the straw hat
and a seersucker smile.
The Cal Trimmer lines
cross like infield grass,
the new couple wear Bermudas,
his shirt is plaid, her silk top
as cool as condensation
on a martini glass. The hostess
knows the havoc of summer,
the dangers of a thin waist
and a striking ass.

What Muriel Taught Jim and Jim Taught Me

The small boy with the hair like startled sleep
sits near the girl who looks to the floor
when you call her name. The boy's voice
is crystal, all edges and angles squeaking
more than he should to stay invisible.
She is no voice at all.
They sit near the door away from the others,
away from the whispers and laughter.
These faces never advertise back to school clothes.
They have no special classes to please their parents.
Their parents look like them, hold quiet places,
cross the sight of the living and make no name.

And you, you call the boy by name.
His is the second you know by heart.
The girl with no voice has a name
you say in a way others memorize its sound.
By the time of the rains, they will remember
your room all their lives. They will keep it
safe like a favorite letter read again and again.
In June they will leave, these two and others.

On Lunch Duty, the Principal Considers Intelligent Design

~~~

S. folds himself like a blue heron
at the table near the stage.
If he weren't all legs, he'd be feet.
The odds for mercy may improve,
might let him stand years from here
an armistice between torso and limbs,
the memory of middle school faded.
Grant him the recall of the one kid
who said hello in passing,
the secretary who offered sanctuary
when the thought of PE
froze him in the front office.
A boy alone is feathers to ruffle
and bones hollowed for flight
when a cloud covers him fast as a fist.

November rain packs the cafeteria.
Summer dissolves into winter
The principal still has a beach chair
in his trunk, collapsed, rods bent,
its folded body a marvel of design
put away for another season.
Someone who survived middle school
imagined featherweight legs
with ample strength and pliant joints
draped in fabric as sturdy as hide.
No one's doing lab work on mercy,
no engineer turns this boy to nylon.

The Hoop in Wallace Stevens' Backyard
for Casey Fuller

On his pilgrimage to Hartford,
Casey dusts snow from the plaque
about snow, peeks in the windows,
though the surprise is the hoop
and half court in the back yard.
When he scrapes clean the foul line,
he discovers someone's painted white feet,
the right foot slightly forward.
Casey's black Chuck Taylor's fit
with inches to spare, lousy in snow
they are perfect for his pantomime
at the line, and once he settles his feet,
he bends at the waist and sees
the white circle with *three bounces*
printed in its center-black like *Wilson*.
The black backboard unusual, though
in winter, in snow, a blackboard
is what he knows, and he dribbles
the imaginary ball three times on the spot.
No one stenciled *exhale* near the line,
still he works each step like a program,
the cloud of his breath is moving
and his legs, chest, arms and hands rise
together, follow through, his shot
rising over the circle of the rim,
the beauty of its perfection,
the whistling of the twine just after.

Custodians

for Jon Graham

⌒‿⌒

The custodian leaves a note:
The storage shed is full.
Each letter distinctly cut,
his mark those typewriter g's.
He wears a backpack vacuum,
listens to swing on headphones,
skips the poems in his *New Yorker*.
His keys fail to jangle like a movie janitor,
though he tells me stories about John Garfield.
He lives downtown close to the library.
He's swing shift. Life restarts here early afternoon.
He shares a recipe with the office women,
and the room smells of ribs simmering,
potato salad with three types of onions.
I hear ice sliding into ice after someone
frees a cold beer from the galvanized tub
as he describes watching the parade from his house.
His voice is whisky and cigarettes,
and I walk into the cartoon of my job
when I accidentally interrupt his smoke
behind the dumpster, caught, and he laughs,
holds the cigarette cupped behind his back
as we both did between classes in the sixties.
Days before he crushes his finger moving tables,
he reviews the remake of *War of the Worlds*.
He waves both hands, ten digits intact,
as he describes the special effects,
praises non-stop action.
In consideration for my biases, he says,
Anyone could have played Cruise's part.

On lunch duty, the movie game runs in my head.
Harry Dean Stanton plays the custodian.
He'll need to put on a couple of pounds.
Today's scene—the parent phone call:
The custodian called my son a little son of a bitch.
Jeff Bridges plays me—it's my movie.
JB calls Harry into the office. It's five p.m.
JB says: Sit. I got a phone call.
Harry laughs, embarrassed.
He says: Sorry, Boss, kid kicked the sink.
The little son of a bitch.
Camera pulls back.
Scene fades with laughter.
The lunch lady snatches a sixth grader's tray,
he is a dollar short in his lunch account.
She plays herself. It's no movie.
This is my mess to clean up.

Voucher

The Spokane River drives its black path
through the city. The gray sky sifts flurries,
a woman changes the weather.
She hints blond and wears the soft touch
of black leather. Jacket and river cut
dark. She is foreground, a wash of color
and clarity in a January morning.
Her hand is in my hand.
She teaches first grade. She says
she and her husband farm near Wilson Creek.

School's out, morning breaks warm.
The screen door slams.
Her husband's a cloud of dust on the horizon.
Their son holds the rope swing in willow shade.
She's lost the black stockings,
her skin's a month of sun,
her jeans lighter than her eyes.
Two days later, I find her on the map
sixty miles north of what I thought nowhere.
I trace the thin blue trickle of Wilson Creek,
follow its turns into the thicker blue vein
Crab Creek assumes in the Channeled Scablands.
No water is small water in flat land. I weave
vessels of leaves and wishes, twist twigs and misses,
return what surfaces to the chance of current.

He Nails His Poems to the Cabin

Yellow jackets love the one for her
so much they pit and pock it
into a jumble of consonants and vowels.
Beneath a line, parts of another emerge.
The poem has no decoy of meat
or fish to temper their revision.
They take the open face of his words
and hang them in the canopy of maples,
make home a lantern so light
love hums through thin walls.
What he wrote for her is paper again,
the lace left pinned to cedar
ruffles in the accident of parting.

About the Author

KEVIN MILLER has worked in the public schools of Washington State for thirty-six years. Miller has taught in public schools in Blaine, Gig Harbor, and Olympia, Washington. He currently teaches special education at Washington Middle School in Olympia. In 1990–91 he was a Fulbright Exchange teacher at Grenå Handelsskole, Grenå, Denmark. Miller lives in Tacoma, Washington.

His first collection of poems *Light That Whispers Morning*, from Blue Begonia Press received the Bumbershoot/Weyerhaeuser Publication award in 1994. Blue Begonia Press published his second collection *Everywhere Was Far* in 1998. Miller received an Artist Trust Grant in support of the second collection and a grant from the Tacoma Arts Commission in support of this collection. He was selected to participate in the Jack Straw Writers Program in 2000. Miller's poems appeared in *Weathered Pages*, an anthology from Blue Begonia Press, 2005.

Cover design: Jonas Lerman
Cover photo: Jackson Moran/Technical assistance: Vance Thompson

Books from *Pleasure Boat Studio: A Literary Press*

(Note: Caravel Books is a new imprint of Pleasure Boat Studio: A Literary Press. Caravel Books is the imprint for mysteries only. Aequitas Books is another imprint which includes non-fiction with philosophical and sociological themes. Empty Bowl Press is a Division of Pleasure Boat Studio.)

Listening to the Rhino • Dr. Janet Dallett • $16 • **an aequitas book**
The Shadow in the Water • Inger Frimansson, trans. by Laura Wideburg • $18 •
 a caravel book
Working the Woods, Working the Sea • Eds. Finn Wilcox & Jerry Gorsline • $22
 • **an empty bowl book**
Weinstock Among the Dying • Michael Blumenthal • $18
The War Journal of Lila Ann Smith • Irving Warner • $18
The Woman Who Wrote King Lear, and Other Stories • Louis Phillips • $16
Dream of the Dragon Pool: A Daoist Quest • Albert A. Dalia • $18
Good Night, My Darling • Inger Frimansson, trans by Laura Wideburg • $16
 • **a caravel book**
Falling Awake: An American Woman Gets a Grip on the Whole Changing World—
 One Essay at a Time • Mary Lou Sanelli • $15 • **an aequitas book**
Way Out There: Lyrical Essays • Michael Daley • $16 • **an aequitas book**
The Case of Emily V. • Keith Oatley • mystery • $18 • **a caravel book**
Monique • Luisa Coehlo, Trans fm Portuguese by Maria de Vasconcelos and
 Dolores DeLuise • $14
The Blossoms Are Ghosts at the Wedding • Tom Jay • $15 • **an empty bowl book**
Against Romance • Michael Blumenthal • $14
Speak to the Mountain: The Tommie Waites Story • Dr. Bessie Blake • $18 / $26 •
 an aequitas book
Artrage • Everett Aison • $15
Days We Would Rather Know • Michael Blumenthal • $14
Puget Sound: 15 Stories • C. C. Long • $14
Homicide My Own • Anne Argula • $16
Craving Water • Mary Lou Sanelli • $15
When the Tiger Weeps • Mike O'Connor • 15
Wagner, Descending: The Wrath of the Salmon Queen • Irving Warner • $16
Concentricity • Sheila E. Murphy • $14
Schilling, from a study in lost time • Terrell Guillory • $16
Rumours: A Memoir of a British POW in WWII • Chas Mayhead • $16
The Immigrant's Table • Mary Lou Sanelli • $14
The Enduring Vision of Norman Mailer • Dr. Barry H. Leeds • $18
Women in the Garden • Mary Lou Sanelli • $13.95
Pronoun Music • Richard Cohen • $16
If You Were With Me Everything Would Be All Right • Ken Harvey • $16
The 8th Day of the Week • Al Kessler • $16
Another Life, and Other Stories • Edwin Weihe • $16
Saying the Necessary • Edward Harkness • $14
Nature Lovers • Charles Potts • $10
In Memory of Hawks, & Other Stories from Alaska • Irving Warner • $15
The Politics of My Heart • William Slaughter • $13
The Rape Poems • Frances Driscoll • $13
When History Enters the House: Essays from Central Europe • Michael Blumenthal
 • $15
Setting Out: The Education of Lili • Tung Nien • Trans fm Chinese by
 Mike O'Connor • $15

Our Chapbook Series:

No. 1: *The Handful of Seeds: Three and a Half Essays* • Andrew Schelling • $7
No. 2: *Original Sin* • Michael Daley • $8
No. 3: *Too Small to Hold You* • Kate Reavey • $8
No. 4: *The Light on Our Faces: A Therapy Dialogue* • Lee Miriam Whitman Raymond
• $8
No. 5: *Eye* • William Bridges • $8
No. 6: *Selected New Poems of Rainer Maria Rilke* • Trans fm German by Alice Derry
• $10
No. 7: *Through High Still Air: A Season at Sourdough Mountain* • Tim McNulty • $9
No. 8: *Sight Progress* • Zhang Er, Trans fm Chinese by Rachel Levitsky • $9
No. 9: *The Perfect Hour* • Blas Falconer • $9
No. 10: *Fervor* • Zaedryn Meade • $10

From other publishers (in limited editions):

Desire • Jody Aliesan • $14 • an empty bowl book
Deams of the Hand • Susan Goldwitz • $14 • an empty bowl book
Lineage • Mary Lou Sanelli • $14 • an empty bowl book
The Basin: Poems from a Chinese Province • Mike O'Connor • $10 • an empty
bowl book
The Straits • Michael • $10 • an empty bowl book
In Our Hearts and Minds: The Northwest and Central America • Ed. Michael Daley
• $12 • an empty bowl book
The Rainshadow • Mike O'Connor • $16 • an empty bowl book
Untold Stories • William Slaughter • $10 • an empty bowl book
In Blue Mountain Dusk • Tim McNulty • $12.95 • a broken moon book
China Basin • Clemens Starck • $14 • a Story Line Press book
Journeyman's Wages • Clemens Starck • $11 • a Story Line Press book

Orders:

Pleasure Boat Studio books are available by order from your bookstore, directly from PBS,
or through the following:

SPD (Small Press Distribution) Tel. 800-869-7553, Fax 510-524-0852
Partners/West Tel. 425-227-8486, Fax 425-204-2448
Baker & Taylor Tel. 800-775-1100, Fax 800-775-7480
Ingram Tel. 615-793-5000, Fax 615-287-5429
amazon.com or **barnesandnoble.com**

Pleasure Boat Studio: A Literary Press
201 West 89th Street
New York, NY 10024
Tel: 212-362-8563 / Fax: 888-810-5308
www.pleasureboatstudio.com / *pleasboat@nyc.rr.com*